TRANSFORMING ANXIETY

The Heart Math Solution for Overcoming, Grow Resilience, Confidence and Conquer Anxious Thoughts

Luis f. Jake

Table of Contents

CHAPTER ONE
INTRODUCTION
Knowing About Anxiety

Anxiety's Nature

Anxiety is a normal reaction to pressure or something that seems dangerous. It's an emotion that ranges in severity from mild to severe and is characterized by anxiety, worry, or unease. Anxiety can be beneficial in some circumstances by increasing awareness or helping people prepare for obstacles, but excessive or continuous anxiety can cause problems. Occasional anxiety is a normal part of life.

Anxiety Disorder Types

The hallmarks of generalized anxiety disorder (GAD) are excessive worry and stress about a variety of life events, frequently without a clear trigger.

An abrupt, strong panic attack coupled with physical symptoms including perspiration, rapid heartbeat, and trouble breathing is known as panic disorder.

An intense fear of social circumstances that causes avoidance of social contacts is known as social anxiety disorder.

Extreme dread of particular things or circumstances, such as spiders, flying, heights, etc., is known as a specific phobia.

The symptoms of obsessive-compulsive disorder (OCD) include intrusive thoughts known as obsessions that cause compulsive activities known as compulsions.

Following exposure to a traumatic event, post-traumatic stress disorder (PTSD) may develop. Symptoms may include flashbacks, nightmares, and excruciating anxiety.

Anxiety's Effects

Many facets of life can be profoundly impacted by anxiety, including:

Physical Health: Prolonged worry can result in physical health concerns such as reduced immune responses, headaches, tense muscles, and digestive troubles.

Mental Health: Substance addiction, depression, and other mental health issues can all be influenced by persistent anxiety.

Work and Relationships: Anxiety can lead to avoidance or difficulty in social situations, which can impair performance at work or school and strain relationships.

Quality of Life: It may make daily living more difficult and reduce overall life satisfaction.

The Anxiety Physiology

Chemistry of the Brain:

Anxiety disorders may be exacerbated by imbalances in neurotransmitters, such as norepinephrine, dopamine, and serotonin.

Amygdala: This brain region is involved in the "fight or flight" response and is responsible for processing emotions. Anxiety may rise as a result of amygdala overactivity.

Hormonal Reaction:

Stress Hormones: In response to stress or perceived dangers, the body releases stress hormones such as cortisol and adrenaline to prime the body for action. Anxiety disorders may be exacerbated by prolonged exposure to these hormones.

Environment and Genetics:

Genetics: Research indicates that anxiety disorders may have a genetic component, but environmental factors are also quite important.

Life Experiences: The chance of getting an anxiety disorder may be raised by traumatic experiences or ongoing pressures.

Cognitive Elements:

Thought Patterns: Anxiety is exacerbated by faulty or negative thought patterns. Cognitive distortions include things like mind reading, overgeneralization, and catastrophizing.

In order to treat anxiety, a variety of therapies—such as cognitive-behavioral therapy (CBT), medication, lifestyle modifications, and stress management techniques—that are customized to each patient's requirements and circumstances are frequently used.

Heart Math's Solution

By emphasizing the relationship between the heart, mind, and emotions, the Heart Math method was created to assist people in managing their stress and emotions. It combines methods designed to bring the heart rate variability (HRV) and the brain into harmony, fostering emotional control and general wellbeing.

Heart Math: The Science of It

Variability in Heart Rate (HRV):

The difference in time between each heartbeat is known as the

HRV. A more flexible and adaptive autonomic nerve system, which is indicative of improved health and stress resilience, is reflected in a higher HRV.

Heart Math aims to achieve coherence, which is a condition in which the heart beat becomes balanced and smooth, causing the heart, brain, and neurological system to synchronize.

The psychophysiology of affect:

Heart-Brain Connection: According to research from the Heart Math Institute, the heart and brain are in communication, affecting cognitive function, emotional experiences, and decision-making.

Emotional Regulation: Heart Math techniques work to control emotions by bringing about a change in the physiological state through coherence-building exercises, focused breathing, and pleasant emotions.

HeartMath Methodologies

1. Heart-Centered Inhalation:

involves using breathing exercises to draw attention to the region surrounding the heart, which encourages coherence and relaxation.

2. The Technique of Quick Coherence:

combines the deliberate creation of good emotions, such as gratitude or concern, with heart-focused breathing to quickly attain coherence.

3. The Freeze-Frame Method:

involves taking a moment to recognize feelings, change to a pleasant emotional state, and mentally reframe stressful situations.

4. Technology of Inner Balance:

Heart Math provides real-time HRV feedback through wearable technologies and apps, assisting users in achieving coherence through breathing and happy feelings.

Applying Heart Math Methods

How to Put Heart Math Techniques Into Practice:

Learn to Breathe with Your Heart in Mind: Engage in breathing exercises that direct attention toward your heart.

Practice Often: Heart Math strategies are more successful in managing stress and emotions when they are regularly practiced.

Real-Time input: To inform coherence-building procedures, make use of technology (if available) that offers real-time input on HRV.

Apply strategies in Daily Life: To help you relax and become more coherent in stressful situations, try using strategies like Quick Coherence or Freeze-Frame.

Combine with Other Practices: Heart Math can be used in conjunction with other stress-reduction methods such as cognitive-behavioral approaches, mindfulness, and meditation.

CHAPTER TWO
Overcoming Anxiety and Fear

1. Recognizing Your Stressors

Identify Patterns: Keep an eye out for circumstances, ideas, or occurrences that frequently cause anxiety or terror.

Maintain a Journal: To learn more about your triggers, note the events that set you off as well as your feelings when they do.

Physical Reactions: Pay attention to how your body responds to triggers, such as elevated heart rate and perspiration.

2. Changing the Way You Think

Cognitive restructuring involves confronting unreasonable or pessimistic ideas that are linked to anxiety or dread.

Checking Reality: Evaluate if your worries are legitimate. Consider whether your concerns are founded in reality or in conjecture.

Reframe situations in a more positive or balanced light by practicing positive reframing.

3. Controlling Your Feelings

Techniques for Mindfulness and Relaxation: To soothe your body and mind, engage in progressive muscle relaxation, mindfulness, deep breathing, or meditation.

Emotional Control: Recognize and categorize your feelings. After giving yourself permission to feel them without passing judgment, learn coping mechanisms for intense feelings, such as grounding exercises.

Seek Assistance: Seek advice and assistance in handling your feelings and anxieties by speaking with friends, family, or a therapist.

Strategies for Transformation

1. The use of exposure therapy

Gradual Exposure: Begin with less upsetting circumstances and work your way up to exposing yourself to triggers in a systematic and controlled manner.

Desensitization: Repeated exposure to a trigger over time might lessen the fear reaction linked to that particular trigger.

2. Methods of Behavior

Relaxation Training: Acquire the skills necessary to combat the bodily manifestations of anxiety.

Reaction Prevention: Steer clear of actions that exacerbate or sustain your anxiety in order to prevent feeding fear.

3. Behavioral-Cognitive Techniques

Thought Logs: Document anxious or frightened thoughts, confront them, and swap them out with more practical and uplifting ideas.

Establish attainable objectives to progressively face anxieties or fears while acknowledging accomplishments along the way.

Putting Changes Into Practice:

Consistency: Make it a habit to routinely detect triggers, alter thinking, and control emotions.

It takes time to get over anxiety and dread, so be patient and persistent. Remain persistent in using these techniques and have patience with yourself.

Self-Care: To support general mental well-being, give self-care activities like exercise, enough sleep, and a balanced diet first priority.

Recall that conquering anxiety and fear is a process that calls for commitment and hard work. Consulting with therapists or counselors who specialize in anxiety disorders might help you receive extra tactics and support that are customized to meet your requirements.

Establishing Calm

1. Developing Inner Calm

Meditation and mindfulness: Engage in mindfulness exercises to maintain present-moment awareness and appreciation. Inner serenity and mental calmness can be developed with meditation.

Gratitude: Pay attention to what you have to be thankful for. Keeping a gratitude diary or thinking back on your life's blessings might help you change your perspective and find contentment.

Practice self-compassion by being nice and understanding to

yourself. Refrain from self-criticism and take care of yourself.

Simplify Your Life: You might feel more at ease and at peace if you simplify your daily activities and declutter your physical area.

2. Strengthening Your Connections

Effective Communication: Listen intently and communicate honestly and freely. Steer clear of assumptions and ask for clarification when necessary.

Empathy and Understanding: Try to put yourself in other people's situations and try to comprehend their feelings and points of view.

Boundaries: To guarantee respect for one another and safeguard your wellbeing, set up appropriate boundaries in partnerships.

Spending quality time with loved ones and participating in joyful activities that promote connection should be your first priority.

3. Leading a Harmonious Life

Maintain a work-life balance by drawing boundaries between your personal and professional lives and making time for hobbies, leisure, and social interactions.

Good Lifestyle Practices: Engage in regular exercise, consume a balanced diet, get enough sleep, and learn stress-reduction methods like yoga or deep breathing.

Interests and Passions: Take part in things that make you happy and fulfilled. To be balanced, follow your passions or hobbies outside of the workplace.

Self-Reflection and Adjustment: Examine your priorities, aspirations, and life on a regular basis. Modify your way of living to reflect what makes you happy and content.

Putting Changes Into Practice:

Regularity and Consistency: Create routines that are dependable and support a healthy lifestyle, nourishing relationships, and inner serenity.

Adaptability: Have the willingness to change tactics as necessary. You may not always benefit from what works for others, so figure out what best suits your requirements and personality.

Seeking Support: Seek advice from mentors, life coaches, or therapists if necessary. They can offer valuable perspectives and strategies to improve balance and tranquility in life.

In order to create peace, you must take care of your inner self, cultivate wholesome connections, and lead a healthy lifestyle. In order to build peace and harmony in all areas of life, one must be attentive, self-aware, and make intentional efforts. This is a constant journey.

THE END